FORDYCE V. HARRIS AND FELSON

Seventh Edition

Case File

Trial Materials

FORDYCE V. HARRIS AND FELSON

Seventh Edition

Case File

Trial Materials

(A companion file to *State v. Harris*)

Laurence M. Rose
Professor of Law Emeritus
University of Miami School of Law
Coral Gables, Florida

An adaptation of *Fordyce v. Harris and Felson*

Originally written by Abraham P. Ordover

NITA®
NATIONAL INSTITUTE FOR TRIAL ADVOCACY

Address inquiries to:
Reprint Permission
National Institute for Trial Advocacy
1685 38th Street, Suite 200
Boulder, CO 80301-2735
Phone: (800) 225-6482
Fax: (720) 890-7069
Email: permissions@nita.org

ISBN 978-1-60156-878-6
eISBN 978-1-60156-879-3

FBA 1878
eFBA 1879

14 13 12 11 10 9 8 7 6 5 4 3

Printed in the United States of America

Official co-publisher of NITA.
WKLegaledu.com/NITA

CONTENTS

Acknowledgments

The original *Fordyce v. Harris and Felson* file was written by Abraham P. Ordover, one of the early authors of NITA case files and a former program director and faculty member. The passage of time and changes in case strategies have been addressed in these revisions, primarily to further the teaching goals and for skill development. This file is designed to be used in a trial advocacy program, either as skill exercises or a final trial or both. Along with its companion, *State v. Harris*, this case file can be effectively used to highlight the differences between civil and criminal advocacy techniques, as well as the effect of the different burdens of proof.

This file is dedicated to all of those who have contributed to the teaching of advocacy and the promotion of the profession.

Laurence M. Rose
Professor of Law Emeritus
Superior, Colorado

INTRODUCTION

The plaintiff, Henry C. Fordyce, brought this action against the defendants, Gerald J. Harris and Edward Felson, seeking damages for their alleged assault and battery on him.

Fordyce alleges that on March 2, YR-1, he was with a friend, Eva Marie Long, having a few drinks at Gus's Bar & Grill in Nita City. At about 11:00 p.m., Harris and Felson entered the bar and sat down at a nearby table. Fordyce claims that they began leering at Ms. Long and later made insulting remarks to her and Fordyce. A fight broke out; the police arrived and restored order. There were no serious injuries and no charges were brought.

Later that evening, according to the plaintiff, when he was on his way home and near an alley about fifty feet from the bar, he was attacked by the defendants. Harris allegedly hit him with a broom handle and Felson allegedly stomped on him with his boots.

The plaintiff was hospitalized with a fractured skull and has completely recovered. His medical bills were $78,052, and he lost wages of $21,000. The medical bills are included as Exhibits A through D.

The defendants deny they assaulted Fordyce. Felson says Fordyce started the fight in the bar and that after the police came, Harris drove Felson directly to his motel. Harris agrees that Fordyce was the aggressor in the bar, and contends he drove Felson to his motel, went to his office, and then went to go see his girlfriend. The police reports, prior arrest records, and pictures of the broomstick are included as Exhibits 1 through 17.

Pretrial discovery has been completed. The applicable law is contained in the proposed jury instructions set forth at the end of the case file.

All years in these materials are stated in the following form:

YR-0 indicates the actual year in which the case is being tried (i.e., the present year);

YR-1 indicates the next preceding year (please use the actual year);

YR-2 indicates the second preceding year (please use the actual year);

Earlier years are sequentially increased.

Electronic exhibits for this case file can be downloaded from the following website:

http://bit.ly/1P20Jea
Password: Fordyce7

SPECIAL INSTRUCTIONS FOR USE AS A FULL TRIAL

When this case file is used as the basis for a full trial, subject to the instructor's discretion, each side should prepare and call the listed four witnesses. If the instructor varies these instructions, the party listed below should select and prepare the witness. For the purposes of pretrial proceedings, the defendants chose to pursue a joint defense.

Plaintiff

Henry Fordyce

Eva Marie Long

Peyton Logan

Melissa Angel

Defendants

Edward Felson

Gerald Harris

Glenda Barkan

Ben Sanders

STIPULATIONS

The parties have agreed to the following stipulations:

1. In Nita City, at the time of the alleged incident, the Late Movie was one and one-half hours in length and was broadcast from 11:30 p.m. to 1:00 a.m.

2. All documents contained in the case file are authentic.

3. The hospital records were made and kept in the regular course of the hospital's business and satisfy all of the requirements of the business records exception to the hearsay rule.

4. The records of the U.S. Department of Agriculture, Forest Service, were made and kept in the regular course of the department's business and satisfy all the requirements of the business records and public records exceptions to the hearsay rule.

IN THE SUPERIOR COURT OF
DARROW COUNTY, NITA
CIVIL DIVISION

HENRY C. FORDYCE,   )
)

Plaintiff,   )
)   COMPLAINT

v.   )
)

GERALD J. HARRIS and   )   487-CV-1253
EDWARD FELSON,   )
)

Defendants.   )

Plaintiff, for his claim against Defendants, alleges:

FIRST CLAIM FOR RELIEF

1. At all times hereinafter mentioned, Plaintiff was, and still is, a resident of Darrow County, Nita.

2. At all times hereinafter mentioned, Defendants were, and still are, residents of Darrow County, Nita.

3. On or about March 2, YR-1, at approximately 11:30 p.m., at or near 2847 Founders Boulevard, Nita City, Nita, Defendant Harris struck Plaintiff on the side of the head with an object. Plaintiff fell to the ground and was hit again by Defendant Harris.

4. On or about March 2, YR-1, at approximately 11:30 p.m., at or near 2847 Founders Boulevard, Nita City, Nita, Defendant Felson stomped on Plaintiff with his boots while Plaintiff was on the ground, already injured from the attack by Defendant Harris.

5. As a result of the actions of both Defendants, Plaintiff suffered a fractured skull and traumatic brain injury, was hospitalized, required extensive therapy and follow-up visits with specialists, and experienced nausea, dizziness, and pain and suffering for several months.

6. As a further result of the actions of both Defendants, Plaintiff was required to be hospitalized, incurred medical and hospital bills, and was unable to work for a period of four months.

SECOND CLAIM FOR RELIEF

7. Plaintiff realleges paragraphs 1 through 6.

8. The actions of Defendant Harris alleged in paragraph 3 were malicious.

9. The actions of Defendant Felson alleged in paragraph 4 were malicious.

WHEREFORE, Plaintiff prays for judgment against Defendants and each of them in the amount of $250,000 in actual damages and $1,000,000 in punitive damages, together with the costs of this action, and for such other and further relief as is just and proper.

Jury Demand

Plaintiff demands a trial by jury in this action.

Packer & Thacker by:

Susan Thacker

SUSAN THACKER
Attorney for Plaintiff
203 North Church Street
Nita City, Nita 99991
(721) 555-2306

Return of Summons

I hereby certify that the above Complaint and Summons were personally served on Edward Felson and Gerald J. Harris on September 4, YR-1.

Wally Dee

Wally Dee
Process Server

IN THE SUPERIOR COURT OF
DARROW COUNTY, NITA
CIVIL DIVISION

HENRY C. FORDYCE,	)	
	)	
Plaintiff,	)	
	)	ANSWER OF DEFENDANT
v.	)	GERALD J. HARRIS
	)	
GERALD J. HARRIS and	)	487-CV-1253
EDWARD FELSON,	)	
	)	
Defendants.	)	

Defendant Gerald J. Harris, for his answer to Plaintiff's complaint:

1. Admits the allegations contained in paragraphs 1 and 2 of Plaintiff's complaint.

2. Denies the allegations in paragraphs 3 and 8 of Plaintiff's complaint.

3. Is without sufficient knowledge or information to form a belief as to the truth of the averments of paragraphs 4, 5, 6, and 9 of Plaintiff's complaint and, therefore, denies the same.

WHEREFORE, Defendant demands judgment in his favor, together with the costs and disbursements of this action.

> McGuire & Russell
> by:
>
> *David McGuire*
>
> DAVID MCGUIRE
> Attorney for Defendant Harris
> 2700 South Jewell Avenue
> Nita City, Nita 99993
> (721) 555-5609

Certificate of Service

I hereby certify that on September 20, YR-1, a copy of the above Answer was sent by facsimile, electronic mail, and placed in the United States mail, postage prepaid, addressed to Susan Thacker, Packer & Thacker, 203 North Church Street, Nita City, Nita 99991.

Alice Michaelson

Alice Michaelson
2700 South Jewell Avenue
Nita City, Nita 99993

IN THE SUPERIOR COURT OF
DARROW COUNTY, NITA
CIVIL DIVISION

HENRY C. FORDYCE,   )
)
Plaintiff,   )
)   ANSWER OF DEFENDANT
v.   )   EDWARD FELSON
)
GERALD J. HARRIS and   )   487-CV-1253
EDWARD FELSON,   )
)
Defendants.   )

Defendant Edward Felson, for his answer to Plaintiff's complaint:

1. Paragraphs 1 and 2: Admitted.

2. Paragraphs 4 and 9: Denied.

3. Paragraphs 3, 5, 6, and 8: Defendant Felson is without knowledge or sufficient information to form a belief as to the truth of these allegations and, therefore, denies same and demands proof thereof.

WHEREFORE, Defendant Felson demands judgment in his favor, with costs according to law.

Darrow County Legal Aid
by:

Louise Bellow

LOUISE BELLOW
Attorney for Defendant Felson
Darrow County Legal Aid
203 South Alder Street
Nita City, Nita 99992
(721) 555-7700

Certificate of Service

I hereby certify that on September 17, YR-1, a copy of the above Answer was sent by facsimile, electronic mail, and placed in the United States mail, postage prepaid, addressed to Susan Thacker, Packer & Thacker, 203 North Church Street, Nita City, Nita 99991.

Evelyn Miller

Evelyn Miller
203 South Alder Street
Nita City, Nita 99992

DEPOSITIONS

DEPOSITION OF HENRY FORDYCE[*]
NOVEMBER 1, YR-1

HENRY FORDYCE, the plaintiff, called to testify on deposition by the defendants and having been duly sworn, testified as follows:

1 My name is Henry C. Fordyce. I was born on August 18, YR-25, in Nita City, Nita. My legal
2 residence is with my parents at 1421 Seminole Drive here in Nita City, but I work for the U.S.
3 Department of Agriculture as a forest ranger at Bear Lake National Forest in the western part
4 of Nita. I work twenty days on and get off for five. Most times I come home on my days off.
5
6 I went to the Nita public schools and graduated from Central High in YR-8. I was really
7 interested in biology and the environment. I decided to attend Nita State University in
8 Montrose to try to get a combined degree in forestry and environmental sciences. It's a
9 special program they have.
10
11 I graduated in YR-4 and have been working as a forest ranger since then. My current posi-
12 tion is Senior Forest Ranger. My annual salary is $84,000 plus benefits.
13
14 One of my special interests is resource administration and, in February last year, I was able
15 to get the department to send me to Nita City to attend a month-long seminar on that sub-
16 ject, which was being held at Nita City College. The dates of the seminar were February 11
17 to March 15. I attended classes all day and was living at home with my parents.
18
19 Eva Marie Long is a woman I dated in college. We still see each other socially from time
20 to time when I'm in Nita City. I called her when I first got into town, and on March 2, I
21 went over to her apartment at about 9:45 p.m. I had been at Fenster's Bar with some
22 friends before then because I thought she had said she wouldn't be ready until 10:00 p.m.,
23 although she texted me around 9:15 to see where I was. I had two scotches at Fenster's
24 and watched a pro basketball game on TV.
25
26 Eva Marie and I talked for a while at her apartment, and then she suggested we go have
27 a drink at Gus's, which is a bar near her apartment. I think it is actually called Gus's Bar &
28 Grill. We got there about 10:30 p.m.
29
30 It was really very nice. The music was low enough so we could talk, and we were discussing
31 old times. I hadn't seen her in several months, and it was good to be together again.
32
33 We were seated at the second table in from the door. I was facing the bar and Eva Marie
34 had her back to the bar and the door. We ordered a couple of drinks.

---

[*] The transcript of Fordyce's deposition was excerpted so that only his answers are reprinted here. Assume that this is a true and accurate rendering of those answers.

1 I noticed two really tough-looking guys at about 11:00 p.m. They walked behind Eva Marie,
2 so she couldn't see that they were staring at her. They sat down at the last table from the
3 door, two tables away from us. No one was at the table in between. I didn't recognize
4 either of them, and Eva Marie didn't appear to either.
5
6 A few minutes later, the one who I now know is Harris started leering and ogling at Eva
7 Marie. This time she saw it and was upset. I told Harris to knock it off. He laughed at me
8 and poked the other guy, who I now know is Felson. The two of them really started getting
9 on Eva Marie. I can't remember everything they said, but I remember Harris saying, "Hey
10 honey, drop that stiff and come over here. I'll show you a real good time." I particularly
11 didn't like the way he said "real." Then Felson, I remember this too, said, "I remember you
12 from down on the corner. What's the matter—business bad—too many cops around?"
13
14 Eva Marie started to cry. I was really angry. I went over and grabbed Felson by his shirt, on
15 either side of his neck, and shook him. He fell off his chair, got up, grabbed a beer bottle,
16 and came after me. I dodged his first swing and picked up a chair to protect myself. When
17 he came at me a second time, I used the chair to keep him away. I never hit Felson with
18 the chair. While I was still holding the chair and before I could get it in position to protect
19 myself, Harris punched me in the gut from the other side, and I doubled over. The wind
20 was knocked out of me and I was dizzy. Before they could jump on me and really do some
21 damage, a cop came and broke up the fight. The cop's name was Officer Logan.
22
23 Officer Logan took everybody's name and asked what had happened. When it was all over,
24 he told us he wasn't going to detain us and to go home. I couldn't believe he didn't arrest
25 those guys for what they did.
26
27 Felson and Harris got up and left. I was still a little dazed, so Eva Marie and I stayed around
28 for a few minutes.
29
30 It was about 11:35 p.m. when we left. We walked out the front door, turned left, and
31 walked up Founders Boulevard towards 28th Street. I was walking on the curb side and Eva
32 Marie was on my left.
33
34 We had only gone about fifty feet from the bar when Harris jumped out of a dark alley.
35 He had a broom handle, or that's what it looked like, raised over his head. He knocked Eva
36 Marie over with his body as he jumped out, pulled me into the alley, and clobbered me on
37 my head. I went down and was flat on my back. At this point, I was facing down the alley
38 and he was standing over me, facing the street. The pain was unbelievable. Then Harris hit
39 me with the broom handle again. Things were getting gray, but I remember seeing Felson
40 come over from my right. I felt him stomp on my stomach with his boot, once, then again.
41 Then I finally passed out.
42
43 The next thing I remember I was in the ambulance on the way to the hospital. Eva Marie
45 was with me. She said, "You could have been killed. You shouldn't have tried to protect me
46 in the bar."

1 At the hospital they told me my skull was fractured, but I was lucky and probably wouldn't
2 have any lasting brain damage. I stayed in the hospital for a couple days, and they ran every
3 test in the book. Blood samples, urine samples, CT scans; they never let up. All night long
4 they came in to take my pulse and temperature and make sure I wasn't in a coma. Finally,
5 after a couple days, they let me go home, but I had to follow up with the doctor for a long
6 time. He wouldn't let me go back to work for four months.

7

8 The terrible throbbing pain went away after a few months. While I had it, they gave me all
9 sorts of pain killers, things I'd never heard of, but they didn't do any good. It finally just got
10 better. The dizziness and nausea went away after a week or two. All they gave me for that
11 was some Zofran, and it only helped a little.

12

13 My doctor said because of the nature of my work that I couldn't go back on the job until
14 the headaches improved. I went back to work in early July.

15

16 My salary was $7,000 a month gross, and I missed four months. I was paid for one month
17 because I had two weeks of sick leave and two weeks of vacation coming. I don't remem-
18 ber the exact amounts of my hospital and drug bills, but they were over $75,000.

19

20 I have been arrested a couple of times, but I have never been convicted of anything more
21 than speeding. The arrests were about three months apart and both were in Wolf Creek,
22 Nita, which is not too far from Bear Lake Park, where I work. Sometimes, when I have some
23 time off, I go there instead of coming home to see my parents. The first arrest was when
24 the police came to a party that one of the other rangers had. They came a couple of times
25 and asked us to keep it down. On the third trip back, they came and took us all downtown
26 and arrested everyone. We all stayed in jail overnight, and the next day the charges were
27 dismissed.

28

29 The second arrest was in a bar in Wolf Creek. I had had too much to drink. We had been
30 helping fight a forest fire for two weeks. We had just gotten it under control, and this was
31 my first night off. When the cop came in and told me I'd had enough and ought to go home,
32 I cussed him out pretty badly—or at least that's what the people who were with me say.
33 Frankly, I don't remember any of it. Anyway, the cop says I grabbed him by his uniform
34 while I was doing that. I got a lawyer and the charges were dropped. Apparently the police
35 officer was pretty reasonable about it.

36

37 I got into an argument with Frank Allen, another ranger, about a year ago. He and I had
38 been dating the same waitress at the park's restaurant. He told me not to see her again.
39 I told him that it was not his business to tell her who to see and that as long as she still
40 wanted to see me, I was going to go out with her. There was a little pushing and shoving.
41 No one got hurt and he later apologized.

42

43 I have brought with me the bills you requested. The first is the statement from Memorial
44 Hospital (see Exhibit A). There are also bills from Dr. Mahajan (see Exhibit B) and Dr. Hamp-
45 ton (see Exhibit C) and one from Robineau's Pharmacy (see Exhibit D).

This deposition was taken in the office of the Harris's counsel on November 1, YR-1. This deposition was given under oath and was read and signed by the deponent.

Certified by:

Anne Hall

Anne Hall
Certified Court Reporter (CCR)

Deposition of Eva Marie Long[*]
November 3, YR-1

EVA MARIE LONG, called to testify on deposition by the defendants and having been duly sworn, testified as follows:

1 My name is Eva Marie Long. I'm twenty-five years old. My address is 676 28th Street,
2 Apartment 11B. I've lived at that address for four years. I'm a freelance photographer and
3 model.
4
5 I was born in Racine, Wisconsin, and went to public schools there until my family moved
6 to Montrose, Nita. I finished high school at Montrose High and went on to Nita State. I got
7 an AB in art history in YR-4.
8
9 I first met Henry Fordyce when I was a sophomore in college. Over the next three years we
10 dated occasionally, but mainly we were friends. After college we sent each other Christmas
11 cards and ran into each other once or twice, but never dated.
12
13 I was pleasantly surprised when Henry called me in late February. I can't remember the
14 date, but I do remember he said he was in town for some kind of forest rangers' conven-
15 tion and that he had plenty of time and didn't have to work too hard. We made a date for
16 March 2, which was the first night I was free.
17
18 He was supposed to be at my apartment at 9:00 pm. When he wasn't there by 9:15, I
19 texted him, and he said he was running late. He came by my apartment at about 10:00
20 p.m. I was a little angry that he was so late. He said he'd been drinking with some friends at
21 a local bar and had lost track of the time. He looked loaded, so I asked him how many he'd
22 had. He said, "One or two scotches." My guess is it was more like five or six.
23
24 We stayed at my place for a few minutes, but then left for Gus's Bar & Grill, which is around
25 the corner. I'd say we got there at about 10:15 p.m., but I'm not positive as to the time.
26
27 Gus's was quiet, as usual. That's what I like about it. We sat down at a table that was two
28 tables away from the door. Henry ordered a scotch for himself and a vodka tonic for me.
29 We talked and drank for about forty-five minutes and had just started our second round
30 when some guys came over and sat down two tables over, the one farthest away from the
31 door.
32
33 The guys at that table hadn't been there five minutes when they started making really
34 awful comments about me. I got angry and told them to knock it off. Then one guy yelled
35 out to Henry that I'm a prostitute. I think he actually said "hooker." That was it. I was in
36 tears. Henry got up and started over toward them. The scruffy one grabbed a beer bottle

---

[*] The transcript of Long's deposition was excerpted so that only her answers are reprinted here. Assume that this is a true and accurate rendering of those answers.

1 by the neck. He told Henry if he came one step closer, he'd cut his face off. I tried to help
2 Henry, but one of them threw me to the ground. It's all so confused now.
3
4 I stayed on the floor until the police came. It seems everyone in the place was either in the
5 fight or trying to break it up. The only thing I'm sure of is that at one point the dressy one
6 knocked Henry down with a punch. One other thing: I did hear them screaming to each
7 other. One of them—I couldn't tell which—said, "Kill him."
8
9 A cop arrived and broke things up. He took all our names and addresses, and asked what
10 happened. I found out the dressy one was named Harris and the scruffy one was named
11 Felson. After a while, he told us he wasn't going to make an arrest and that we should all
12 go home. We left about five minutes after Harris and Felson.
13
14 When we left the bar, and before we were even a block away, Harris and Felson jumped
15 out of an alley and clobbered us. I was really startled when they jumped out. The alley
16 was dark, so they just came from nowhere. Harris threw me to the ground. As I was on the
17 ground, I was to Harris's right. He was facing the street, and Henry was facing the alley.
18 Harris had a small pole of some kind, it looked like a broomstick, in his right hand. He hit
19 Henry over the head with it. Henry went down and then Felson started kicking him. The
20 whole time I could see Harris's right profile. I guess it was about five to ten seconds before
21 I started screaming, got up, and ran for help. It was then I saw Felson standing to Harris's
22 left.
23
24 When I came back with a cop, Henry was out cold and all bloodied. Harris and Felson were
25 nowhere to be seen. I could not find my purse or my phone. When the ambulance came,
26 I got in with Henry and the cop followed in his car. On the way to the hospital Henry woke
27 up. He said his head was really hurting and that Felson and Harris had nearly killed him and
28 that they would pay for it.
29
30 At the hospital, I told the police what had happened. A few days later, Officer Logan called
31 me to come down to the police station. I picked Felson and Harris out of a lineup. I knew
32 right when I saw them they were the ones. I later told the police, however, that I couldn't
33 be sure what Felson actually did to Henry. I understand they dropped the charges against
34 both of them. I don't know why. A few days later, I got a call to come to the police station
35 to pick up my purse and phone. Everything was there except about $50 in cash.
36
37 I have had some problems with drugs, but that was all in the past. The last incident was
38 more than a month ago. I was arrested twice for having cocaine. Both times the charges
39 were dismissed. The first time it was because the person who actually owned the stuff con-
40 fessed. The second time the cops lost the evidence. That stuff was a friend's, not mine. The
41 most recent thing was a couple of months ago. I tried using some cocaine, and there must
42 have been something in it because it knocked me right out. They took me to the hospital
43 where they gave me a shot of something and let me go home. The police did question me,
44 but there were no charges. That last incident scared me. After that last time, I learned my
45 lesson. I stopped using it then and haven't used any since.

This deposition was taken in the office of Harris's counsel on November 3, YR-1. This deposition was given under oath and was read and signed by the deponent.

Certified by:

Anne Hall

Anne Hall
Certified Court Reporter (CCR)

DEPOSITION OF EDWARD FELSON[*]
NOVEMBER 15, YR-1

EDWARD FELSON, a defendant, called to testify on deposition by the plaintiff and having been duly sworn, testified as follows:

1   My name is Edward W. Felson. I am twenty-eight years old. I am currently being held in the
2   Nita City Jail on the charge of felony armed robbery (15–30 years) of a liquor store in Nita
3   City in July YR-1. I didn't do it and my lawyer will prove it at trial.
4
5   Gerald Harris is a friend of mine from high school. I haven't really seen him except to say
6   "hi" since then, except for the night we went out to a wrestling show and then to a bar.
7   I know he's got a girlfriend, but I don't remember her name. I met her once a little while
8   before Gerry and I went out, but she didn't seem very friendly. It was like she was too good
9   for me or something.
10
11 On March 2, I was staying at the Eastern Motel and City Taxi headquarters, where I some-
12 times worked. I called to meet Gerry at his office on Founders Boulevard in Nita City. Gerry
13 had done pretty well for himself since high school and owned his own business. I was
14 having a hard time finding a full-time job, so I looked him up. I got to his office at about
15 7:30 p.m. He was finishing up some work, so I just sat around and talked with him. I told
16 him I needed a job and asked if he could help me out. He explained that he had cleaning
17 contracts that didn't allow him to hire convicted felons, so I was out of luck. It seemed to
18 me that Gerry could have made an exception for an old friend, but I guess he's gotten too
19 big for his britches now that he's a fancy businessman. Anyhow, he asked me if I wanted to
20 go out to a wrestling show. He called up his old lady and asked her to come along, but she
21 didn't want to go, so we went to the wrestling show at the Arena, which was about four
22 blocks away.
23
24 After the match, Gerry asked me if I wanted to get a couple of beers on him. I figured if I
25 couldn't get a job, I might as well get a few free beers, so I went along. We went to a joint
26 called Gus's Bar & Grill on Founders Boulevard. It's a neighborhood bar, pretty dark, but
27 with good music. I guess we got there just before 11:00 p.m. We went in the front door and
28 up to the bar. Gerry immediately started hitting on the bartender. She wasn't bad looking
29 and Gerry was trying to get something going for when she got off work. Gerry thinks he's a
30 ladies' man with all his fancy clothes and everything, but near as I can tell, he was making
31 a fool of himself. The bartender must have bought his line though, because she said she'd
32 meet him after work. While this was going on, we had a beer at the bar.
33
34 After Gerry got his promise from the lady, we moved to a table with two chairs in the back
35 part of the bar. It was the one nearest the booths. I was sitting with my back to the bar

---

[*] The transcript of Felson's deposition was excerpted so that only his answers are reprinted here. Assume that this is a true and accurate rendering of those answers.

1   and Gerry was facing the bar, still making eyes at the bartender. I looked to my right and
2   saw a working girl I recognized. She usually was hustling guys out on Founders Boulevard.
3   I was just telling Gerry about this when this guy who smelled like a damned distillery comes
4   flying at me and knocks me off my chair. He also hit the table and spilled a beer on Gerry.
5
6   I got up and started mixing it up with him. He was obviously pretty drunk, but when he
7   picked up a chair, I got a little scared. I don't care what anybody says, I never picked up a
8   beer bottle and threatened anybody. Gerry must have been mad at the guy for spilling beer
9   on him because he hit the drunk pretty hard in the stomach.
10
11 About that time, a cop came in and broke the thing up. He told us all to cool it and go on
12 home, but first took our names and addresses.
13
14 The fight wasn't any big deal and no one was hurt. Anyway, I didn't want to hassle with the
15 cops. Gerry said he would drive me home in his red Beamer. During the ride, Gerry was
16 still bitching about getting a little beer on him. I told him something like he'd come a long
17 way from high school when he'd have been happy about having a beer to spill. We got to
18 the motel about 11:20, and I left him at the motel office, then went to my room, watched
19 some TV, and went to sleep.
20
21 Two days later, I got busted by the cops at my motel. They said I was under arrest for knock-
22 ing the drunk from the bar upside the head. I told them I didn't have anything to do with
23 it. They searched my room and asked if I had any boots. I told them I don't own any boots,
24 and they didn't find any.
25
26 The next day, they put me in a lineup with Gerry and five other guys. They put me on
27 $5,000 bail. I couldn't make it and big shot Gerry wouldn't bail me out, so I stayed there
28 for two weeks. Then we went to court, and I got a public defender. She got the case dis-
29 missed, and they let me go. I now know the drunk in the bar is named Fordyce, but I never
30 did nothing to him.

This deposition was taken in the office of plaintiff 's counsel on November 15, YR-1. This
deposition was given under oath and was read and signed by deponent.

Certified by:

Roger Davis
Roger Davis
Certified Court Reporter (CCR)

DEPOSITION OF GERALD HARRIS[*]
NOVEMBER 15, YR-1

GERALD HARRIS, a defendant, called to testify on deposition by the plaintiff and having been duly sworn, testified as follows:

1 My name is Gerald J. Harris. I am twenty-seven years old. I live at 24 Wilson Street in Glen-
2 dale, Nita. Glendale is a suburb of Nita City. I currently own Sanders Cleaning Services, Inc.
3 Our office and warehouse are located at 2608 Founders Boulevard in Nita City. I had gotten
4 in some trouble when I was a kid, but got straightened out by my former boss, Ben Sand-
5 ers. I started working for Mr. Sanders right out of high school, and I bought the business
6 from him in YR-3 when he retired. My business does contract cleaning services for various
7 businesses and governmental agencies.
8
9 I recently had some business trouble with some political hacks in the Nita City municipal
10 government. They made some claims that I had been overcharging for the services I per-
11 form for the city, but their allegations are totally unfounded. It's all been cleared up now.
12 The business is going very well. I employ over one hundred people, and last year the busi-
13 ness grossed $2,000,000. You don't make that kind of money by overcharging the city, or
14 anyone else for that matter. That kind of reputation can kill you in this business.
15
16 I am single, but I have a steady girlfriend. Her name is Glenda Barkan. She lives in Apart-
17 ment 22 at 522 Grace Avenue in Nita City.
18
19 On March 2, I got a call at work from an old high school friend of mine, Eddie Felson.
20 I hadn't spent any time with Eddie since high school, although I'd seen him around from
21 time to time. He said he was staying at the Eastern Motel, and he asked if we could get
22 together that night, so I arranged for him to meet me at the office at about 7:30 p.m. I was
23 working late that night, as I do most every night, being that I'm the CEO for my business.
24
25 Eddie showed up a little early, and we sat around and talked for a while. He was looking for
26 a job, so we talked about what he'd been up to for the past couple of years. It turned out
27 that he'd had some trouble with the law and was convicted of a couple of crimes. I told him
28 that unfortunately, given the fact that I had a number of cleaning contracts with the state,
29 local, and federal governments, I wasn't allowed to have any convicted felons on my staff.
30 He seemed a little disappointed, but said that he understood.
31
32 I suggested we go out and see a wrestling match at the Arena, a few blocks away. I called
33 Glenda, but she said she had some work to do and told me to come over later that evening.
34 She had met Eddie once before, but he seemed to rub her the wrong way. We went to the
35 Arena and saw three or four matches. I didn't care for the wrestling, but Eddie seemed to

---

* The transcript of Harris's deposition was excerpted so that only his answers are reprinted here. Assume that this is a true and accurate rendering of those answers.

1   really get off on the fights and kicking. We left a little after 10:30 p.m., and we decided to
2   go down to Gus's Bar & Grill, which is about a block away from my office. I felt bad about
3   not being able to help Eddie out with a job, so I figured the least I could do was take him
4   out for beer.
5
6   We got to Gus's at about 10:45 p.m. or so. Even though it's only about a block from my
7   office, I really don't hang out there. I had been there only a couple of times before. It's a
8   little bit of a dive, always dark and smelly. When we got to Gus's, we went up to the bar to
9   order a couple of beers. The barmaid there was kind of cute, and I was kidding her about
10   taking her out sometime. I think I asked her what time she got off work and whether she
11   would go out with me, but I was only joking. It was just talk and she knew it. As I said, I had
12   a date to meet my girlfriend later that night.
13
14   We had a beer at the bar and then took our second to a table. There were four tables with
15   two chairs in the room, and we went to the one all the way in the back of the room. I was
16   sitting facing the bar, and Eddie was sitting with his back to the bar.
17
18   We looked over, and one table away was a really good looking woman and a guy who
19   looked like he was smashed. Eddie told me she was a hooker. He started giving her the eye
20   when all of a sudden the drunk, who I now know to be the plaintiff, Fordyce, comes flying
21   across the room and knocks Eddie to the floor. He also hit our table and spilled some beer
22   on me, but it was no big deal. I went after the drunk just to break up the fight. The woman
23   was involved somehow, but I just pushed her aside. I never saw Eddie with a beer bottle in
24   his hand, but it all happened so quick, he could have had one.
25
26   We were wrestling around on the floor when a cop came in and broke up the fight. He told
27   us to take it easy and just go home, but first took our names and addresses. To tell you the
28   truth, I was glad he said that, because it was pretty clear to me that Eddie had changed a
29   whole lot since high school, and I really didn't want to have anything to do with him.
30
31   I agreed to drive Eddie back to his motel. The drunk and the woman were still in the bar.
32   During the ride, Eddie said something like, "I'll teach that guy to beat on me." I told him he
33   should cool it, that the guy was just a drunk and nobody got hurt, so he should just forget it.
34
35   We got to his motel about 11:30, and I left him at the motel office. I then went back to my
36   office and cleaned up a couple of things and then drove over to Glenda's. Her apartment
37   is located about twenty blocks from my office, about two miles away. I got there about
38   midnight. I guess Glenda was sleeping when I got to her apartment because it took her a
39   couple of minutes to answer the door. I would have left, but I heard the TV, so I just waited
40   until she answered the door.
41
42   We sat around for about an hour until the end of the Late Movie and then I went home.
43   I told Glenda about the fight in the bar. She was real upset with me and told me I should
44   grow up. She said something like, "Just because you went out with a friend from high
46   school doesn't mean you have to act like you're still in high school." I told her that I felt

1 sorry for Eddie, but that I guessed she was right about him being a bad apple. I got home
2 at about 1:30 a.m. You can make pretty good time to Glendale when there's no traffic.
3
4 A couple of days later, I got picked up by the cops at my home. They told me that Fordyce,
5 the drunk from Gus's, got beat up outside the bar. I told them it wasn't me or Eddie. The
6 cops put Eddie and me in a lineup. They charged me with assault or something like that
7 and made me post a bond of $5,000 and threatened me with twelve to twenty-five years.
8 A couple of weeks later, I went down to court with my lawyer, and the DA dropped the
9 charges against me. The worst part of the whole thing was that Glenda was so upset.
10
11 Just like I told the cops, I didn't have anything to do with beating up this Fordyce guy. The
12 first and only time I saw him was in Gus's on March 2. I feel sorry for the guy, but I'm not
13 going to pay for something I didn't do.

This deposition was taken in the office of plaintiff's counsel on November 15, YR-1. This
deposition was given under oath and was read and signed by the deponent.

Certified by:

Roger Davis

Roger Davis

Certified Court Reporter (CCR)

DEPOSITION OF PEYTON LOGAN*
DECEMBER 10, YR-1

PEYTON LOGAN, called to testify on deposition by the defendants and having been duly sworn, testified as follows:

1 My name is Peyton C. Logan. I live at 4281 Oceanside Drive in Nita City. My spouse teaches
2 at Nita East Elementary School, and we have two children. Jamie is eight and Alex is four.
3 I'm thirty-four years old and have an associate degree in police sciences from Nita Com-
4 munity College.
5
6 I got out of school when I was twenty, in YR-14. I served three years in the Marines and was
7 honorably discharged in YR-11. After that I worked for several years in my father-in-law's
8 business, a chain of dry-cleaning stores. I started as a clerk, then moved up to manager of
9 the central plant where they do all the actual cleaning. I realized I just wasn't happy being
10 in that business and really wanted to be a police officer. Being a cop was something I'd
11 wanted to do ever since I was a kid. My uncle was a police officer, so I think that's where I
12 got the idea.
13
14 I started at the Nita City Police Academy in YR-6. It was a six-month program, and I finished
15 first in my class. Since then I have been a patrol officer. I recently took the sergeant's exam
16 and scored higher than anyone else. I will get the first opening, which should be in six to
17 ten months.
18
19 On the night of March 2, I was assigned to foot patrol in the area of Gus's Bar. It's a high
20 crime area, and I was part of a special high visibility unit that had been assigned to the
21 area for several months. At 11:00 p.m., I was alerted to a 911 call about a fight in Gus's Bar.
22 I was only a block away. I ran there and entered the bar and found three men going at it.
23 A fourth person, a woman, appeared to be caught in the middle and was hiding under a
24 nearby table. I broke up the fight, separated the people, and took all their names. No one
25 seemed sure how it had happened, and despite some overturned chairs, there wasn't any
26 real damage. I gave them all a warning and told them to go home. I did not issue any cita-
27 tions or arrest anyone.
28
29 When I was on my next loop around the neighborhood heading south on Founders near
30 Gus's at 11:35 p.m., I heard screaming and again encountered the woman who had been
31 under the table. Her name is Eva Marie Long. She came running towards me yelling.
32 I couldn't make out everything she was saying, but I did hear her say, "They're killing my
33 friend." I drew my weapon and ran toward the alley she was pointing to. When I got there,
34 Henry Fordyce was out cold and bleeding badly from his head. I called for an ambulance
35 and a backup unit.

---

* The transcript of Logan's deposition was excerpted so that only the answers are reprinted here. Assume that this is a true and accurate rendering of those answers.

1   When the Memorial Hospital ambulance arrived, I helped them load Fordyce inside. The
2   woman got in with him. Long told me that the assailant used a stick as a weapon and that
3   her purse was missing. I searched the vicinity of the alley and found a stick, like a broom-
4   stick, with what appeared to be blood on it, in a dumpster down the alley. I photographed
5   it and placed it in an evidence bag. I also found a purse, wallet, and phone on the ground
6   next to the dumpster. I photographed them and placed them in evidence bags. I took the
7   evidence bags with me. I also looked for surveillance cameras in the alley, but there were
8   none. I rode to Memorial Hospital in the backup vehicle, which arrived about the same
9   time as the ambulance. I locked the evidence bags in the trunk of the backup vehicle.
10

11   At the hospital, Long told me she and Fordyce had been attacked by the same men who
12   had been in the fight at the bar. When the doctors let me talk to Fordyce, he confirmed
13   her identifications, but he was awfully groggy at the time. I put out a BOLO on Felson and
14   Harris.
15

16   When I got to the police station, I took the evidence bags out of the locked trunk and
17   checked them into the evidence room for further analysis.
18

19   A couple of days later, when they were both under arrest, I scheduled a lineup for Ms.
20   Long. Fordyce was still in the hospital and couldn't participate. She immediately picked out
21   both men. However, when the detectives and I spoke with her later, she indicated she was
22   positive of the Harris ID, but much less sure on Felson. With the weakness of her ID and the
23   fact that Fordyce probably didn't see much—the alley where I found him was very dark—
24   I recommended that the charges be dismissed. They were. A few days later, I received a
25   report from the crime lab on the evidence. The only usable prints on the purse, wallet, and
26   phone were Long's—they were on file. The blood on the stick matched Fordyce, but no
27   usable prints were found.

This deposition was taken in the office of Harris's counsel on December 10, YR-1. This deposition was given under oath, and was read and signed by the deponent.

Certified by:

Anne Hall

Anne Hall
Certified Court Reporter (CCR)

DEPOSITION OF GLENDA BARKAN[*]
DECEMBER 10, YR-1

GLENDA BARKAN, called to testify on deposition by the plaintiff and having been duly sworn, testified as follows:

1   My name is Glenda Barkan. I am twenty-two years old and single. I live in Apartment 22
2   at 522 Grace Avenue in Nita City. I am a senior at Nita University, majoring in history. I'll
3   graduate in June of this year and hope to go on to law school. Gerald Harris is my boy-
4   friend. We have been seeing each other for over a year. Gerald owns a cleaning business
5   called Sanders Cleaning Services, Inc. I guess he does pretty well in the business, but we
6   really don't talk about his work much. He's more interested in what I do at school, probably
7   because he never got a chance to go to college. Depending on where I get into law school,
8   we'll probably get married in a year or so if our relationship stays as good as it's been.
9

10 On March 2, I got a phone call from Gerald at about 7:00 p.m. He was supposed to come
11 over to my apartment that night to watch some TV or listen to music—nothing special, we
12 were just going to spend some time together. He called me to tell me that he was meeting
13 a friend of his named Eddie Felson. Gerald wanted me to go to a wrestling match with him
14 and Felson, but I told him that I had some studying to do, so I would pass. Gerald and I had
15 met Felson one time before and I thought he was a jerk, but Gerald seemed to like him.
16 Gerald told me they had been friends in high school, but he hadn't spent any time with him
17 since then. I was a little upset that Gerald was standing me up, but because I needed to do
18 some reading, I told him to come by when he finished with Felson.
19

20 I finished reading my assignment and turned on the television to catch the 11:00 p.m.
21 news. I must have fallen asleep, because a little later I was awakened by the doorbell. It
22 was Gerald. I don't remember what time it was, but the Late Movie was on when Gerald
23 woke me up. He came in and we talked for a while. He seemed a little upset, so I asked him
24 what was wrong. Gerald told me that Felson had gotten in a fight at some bar over a girl
25 and that he had to break it up. It couldn't have been too serious because he wasn't dishev-
26 eled or bruised at all. I told Gerald that he really should grow up. I don't believe in fighting
27 for any reason, especially a bar fight over some girl.
28

29 Gerald stayed for a while and we talked. The TV was still on, although the volume was way
30 down. I think he left at about 1:00 a.m. because the Late Movie had just ended.
31

32 A couple of days later, Gerald called me and came over. He told me that I was right about
33 Felson, because the guy Felson was fighting got beat up pretty bad and Gerald suspected
34 that Felson did it. He said that he and Felson got arrested that afternoon. I was really upset
35 about the whole thing. Gerald calmed me down and told me not to worry, that he wasn't

---

[*] The transcript of Barkan's deposition was excerpted so that only her answers are reprinted here. Assume that this is a true and accurate rendering of those answers.

1   involved. It turned out all right because the charges were dropped against Gerald. I just
2   hope Gerald has learned his lesson about the kinds of people he should hang out with. I'm
3   sure he had nothing to do with beating up poor Mr. Fordyce. He's just not that kind of man.
4   If he was, I wouldn't have anything to do with him.

This deposition was taken in the office of plaintiff's counsel on December 10, YR-1. This deposition was given under oath and was read and signed by the deponent.

Certified by:

Roger Davis

Roger Davis
Certified Court Reporter (CCR)

DEPOSITION OF MELISSA ANGEL*
DECEMBER 15, YR-1

MELISSA ANGEL, called to testify on deposition by the plaintiff and having been duly sworn, testified as follows:

1   My name is Melissa Angel. I am twenty-seven years old and divorced. I have no kids. I live
2   at 3056 Jackson Avenue, Apartment 301, in Nita City. I'm a bartender at Gus's Bar & Grill at
3   2847 Founders Boulevard in Nita City. Gus's is a small bar that serves food. It's got typical
4   low bar lighting. The music is kept pretty soft for a bar. I've been working there for the past
5   five years.
6
7   On March 2, I was working the night shift, from 4:00 p.m. until midnight. It was a pretty
8   slow night. At about 11:00 p.m., two guys came in and sat at the bar. I later found out they
9   were Gerald Harris and Eddie Felson. They both ordered beers. Harris was all "Mr. Cool"
10 and trying to flirt with me. He kept asking me when I got off work. He was being a real pest.
11 I knew he was probably all talk, but partially to shut him up and partially because he wasn't
12 bad looking, I agreed to go out with him when I got off work at midnight. The other guy,
13 Felson, wasn't saying much, just drinking his beer. The two had a beer at the bar and then
14 took another and moved to a table towards the back.
15
16 A couple of minutes later I came out of the kitchen and a fight had started. It was Harris
17 and Felson wrestling with a guy who had been sitting with a girl at another table. They
18 were fighting near the table where Felson and Harris had been sitting. I don't know how
19 the fight started, but it seemed like Harris was doing a number on the other guy. The cook
20 must have called 911, and a cop—I think his name was Officer Logan—came in and broke
21 up the fight. He didn't arrest anyone, just took their names and told them to leave.
22
23 Harris and Felson left the bar at around 11:20. Fordyce and Ms. Long left about ten min-
24 utes later. I went back to work. A few minutes later, I heard screaming from outside, ran to
25 the door, and saw Long and Fordyce in the alley with Officer Logan. Logan must have called
26 for an ambulance and a backup police unit. The ambulance got there almost immediately.
27 Logan told me that Fordyce got beat up.
28
29 At midnight, when we closed, Harris had not come back to the bar. I figured he'd forgotten
30 me so I left. I left a couple of minutes after twelve. I started walking down the block when I
31 saw a red car with a guy I thought was Harris driving north in front of Gus's down Founders
32 Boulevard.
33
34 I waved and called out to him, but he did not turn or stop. I don't know if anyone else was
35 in the car. I never saw Harris again.

---

* The transcript of Angel's deposition was excerpted so that only her answers are reprinted here. Assume that this is a true and accurate rendering of those answers.

This deposition was taken in the office of plaintiff's counsel on December 15, YR-1. This deposition was given under oath and was read and signed by the deponent.

Certified by:

Roger Davis

Roger Davis
Certified Court Reporter (CCR)

Exhibits

Exhibit A

MEMORIAL HOSPITAL

P.O. Box 9997
Nita City, Nita 99997

Henry C. Fordyce
1421 Seminole Dr.
Nita City, Nita 99990

Statement Date:	Account Number:	Due Date:
April 4, YR-1	YR-105934771	Upon Receipt

Emergency Room (Date of Service: 3/2/YR-1)	$5,900
Private Room Charge (Dates of Service: 3/3/YR-1–3/6/YR-1)	$33,475
X-rays (Dates of Service: 3/2/YR-1–3/3/YR-1)	$1,425
Laboratory (Dates of Service: 3/2/YR-1–3/6/YR-1)	$2,137
Pharmacy (Dates of Service: 3/2/YR-1–3/6/YR-1)	$3,020
Radiology (CT Scan) (Date of Service: 3/3/YR-1)	$5,940
Total:	**$51,897**

Detach here and return bottom portion with payment.

Patient Name:	Account Number:	Amount Paid:
Henry Fordyce	YR-105934771	$

Please do not send cash.
Make checks payable to **Memorial Hospital**

Memorial Hospital
Attention: Patient Accounts
P.O. Box 9997
Nita City, Nita 99997

☐Visa ☐MasterCard ☐American Express ☐Discover

Account No.: _____

Expiration Date: _____ CVV: _____

Signature: _____

MEMORIAL HOSPITAL
PHYSICIAN GROUP

P.O. Box 9942
Nita City, Nita 99997

Henry C. Fordyce
1421 Seminole Dr.
Nita City, Nita 99990

Statement Date:	Account Number:	Due Date:
April 4, YR-1	YR-105934771	Upon Receipt

Emergency Room (Dr. R. Villareal)	$450
Hospitalist (Dr. F.X. Jackson, Dr. L. White)	$2,250
Neurologist (Dr. J. Mahajan)	$4,750
Radiologist (Dr. E. Steinmetz)	$675
Total:	**$8,125**

Detach here and return bottom portion with payment.

Patient Name:	Account Number:	Amount Paid:
Henry Fordyce	YR-105934771	$

Please do not send cash.
Make checks payable to **Memorial Hospital**

Memorial Hospital Physician Group
Attention: Patient Accounts
P.O. Box 9942
Nita City, Nita 99997

☐Visa ☐MasterCard ☐American Express ☐Discover

Account No.: _____

Expiration Date: _____ CVV: _____

Signature: _____

National Institute for Trial Advocacy

Exhibit B

Nita Neurology, Inc.
Jordan Mahajan, MD
2211 Smith Boulevard
Nita City, Nita 99995

8/21/YR-1

Mr. Henry C. Fordyce
1421 Seminole Drive
Nita City, Nita 99990

Account Number: 57834214

Amount Due: $14,400

> Dates of Service
> 3/7/YR-1 through 8/17 YR-1

Date Due: **Upon Receipt**

Patient Name: Henry Fordyce   **Account Number:** 57834214   **Amount Paid:** $_____

Please do not send cash.
Please write account number on check.
Make checks payable to **Nita Neurology, Inc.**

Nita Neurology, Inc.
2211 Smith Blvd.
Nita City, Nita 99995

Exhibit C

Dana Hampton, MD
Hampton Family Practice
1061 Jackson Ave.
Nita City, Nita 99994
(555) 824-5374

Henry C. Fordyce
1421 Seminole Dr.
Nita City, Nita 99990

Statement date: August 2, YR-1

Pay this amount: $1,750

Account number: 32057

Date due: Upon receipt

Date of service:	Description of services provided:	Amount billed:
3/9/YR-1	Office visit	$175
3/16/YR-1	Office visit	$175
3/23/YR-1	Office visit	$175
4/6/YR-1	Office visit	$175
4/20/YR-1	Office visit	$175
5/4/YR-1	Office visit	$175
5/18/YR-1	Office visit	$175
6/1/YR-1	Office visit	$175
6/22/YR-1	Office visit	$175
7/20/YR-1	Office visit	$175
Total due:		**$1,750**

Exhibit D

ROBINEAU'S PHARMACY

2810 North Grace Avenue
Nita City, Nita 99991

August 25, YR-1

Statement of Account

Mr. Henry C. Fordyce
1421 Seminole Drive
Nita City, Nita 99990

For prescriptions filled between March 6, YR-1, and August 3, YR-1 $1,880

TOTAL DUE: **$1,880**

PAST DUE

Please give this matter your prompt attention.

Exhibit 1

Hospital Report for Henry Fordyce

 # MEMORIAL HOSPITAL

PATIENT:	Henry C. Fordyce 1421 Seminole Dr. Nita City, Nita 99990	DOB:	August 18, YR-25
EMPLOYER:	U.S. Dept. of Agriculture Forest Service Regional Office Nita City, Nita 99995	NOK:	Mrs. Stephen Fordyce Same Address
INSURANCE:	Gov't Policy Plan 3/80		
ADMITTED:	3/3/YR-1 3:50 a.m.		

3/2/YR-1 11:50 p.m.	ED—patient arrived via ambulance. Patient alert and oriented to person, place, time, and situation upon arrival to ED. Paramedics report patient was unconscious when they picked him up, reactive to auditory stimuli. Bleeding from scalp, nose, and ears. Upon exam, pupils equal and reactive, though dilated. Patient sensitive to light and sound. Patient reports nausea; vomited in ED; given Zofran. Patient reports having been hit repeatedly with broom handle and kicked several times in abdomen. Tender in lower right quad. Multiple contusions abdomen and pelvic area. Small laceration over right eyebrow; will not require stitches. BP 150/100. Resp. 20. Temp. 98.9. Pulse 80, Pain 8/10. Blood alcohol level .15. Typed and cross-matched. Full skull, spinal, and abdominal plain film series and cranial CT ordered. R. Villareal, MD
3/3/YR-1 12:35 a.m.	Skull, spinal, and abdominal series as per Jones's order. Diagonal fracture on left temporal lobe approximately 3 mm above ear socket. Fracture extends 4 mm diagonally toward left temple. Spinal films negative. Abdominal film negative. Cranial CT grossly normal; shows no swelling, no hemorrhaging. E. Steinmetz, MD, Radiologist

3/3/YR-1 4:20 a.m.	Patient awake complains of restlessness, inability to sleep, sharp pains in area of fracture, general pain in abdominal area, significant nausea. Awake, alert, and oriented x4. Pupils equal and reactive. Significant ataxia observed; patient advised to call nurse for assistance before leaving bed. Morphine IV PRN for pain, Zofran PRN for nausea. BP 120/80, Pulse 80, Resp. 22, Temp. 98.4, Pain 7/10. J. Mahajan, MD
3/3/YR-1 10:30 a.m.	Patient complains of headache and abdominal ache. Patient significantly ataxic with ambulation. Continue IV Morphine and Zofran PRN. F.X. Jackson, MD
3/3/YR-1 1:00 p.m.	Patient asleep; does not awaken to auditory stimuli. Discontinue Morphine IV. BP 120/80, Resp. 20, Temp. 99.2, Pulse 58. F.X. Jackson, MD
3/3/YR-1 6:00 p.m.	Complains of severe sharp headache with sensitivity to light and noise. Continue to monitor for signs of traumatic brain injury. J. Mahajan, MD
3/4/YR-1 12:30 a.m.	Patient awake. Complains of pain in skull area 7/10. Resume Morphine IV. L. White, MD
3/4/YR-1 7:00 a.m.	Patient pain 5/10. Reduce Morphine. Patient awake, alert. Pupils normal. Patient continues to be ataxic and is advised to call nurse for help with ambulation. J. Mahajan, MD
3/4/YR-1 4:00 p.m.	Some improvement noted. Continue Morphine overnight if needed. L. White, MD
3/5/YR-1 7:00 a.m.	Continued improvement. Progress good. Discontinue Morphine. Darvocet as needed. Could discharge tomorrow if progress continues. Patient will not be able to drive due to head injury; will need to arrange rides to follow-up appointments. Social worker will assist with securing transportation. L. White, MD
3/5/YR-1 4:30 p.m.	Patient pain 6/10. Pupils equal and reactive. Ataxia resolved; patient ambulatory without assistance, though he complains of dizziness and nausea. Continued pain in head, continued sensitivity to light and sound. Begin Imitrex for headache pain. Continue Zofran PRN for nausea and vomiting. J. Mahajan, MD

3/6/YR-1 7:30 a.m.	Transportation arranged for patient by social worker. Discharged to home with orders to follow up with neurology in two days, follow up with primary physician for pain and nausea control, begin physical and massage therapy in two weeks to help alleviate headaches.
	L. White, MD
	J. Mahajan, MD

Certified as a true and correct copy of permanent records of Memorial Hospital, Nita City, Nita.

Sherman Fox

Sherman Fox

Director, Medical Records Memorial Hospital

Exhibit 2

Forest Service Letter

United States Department of Agriculture

Forest Service
Nita Regional Office
Nita City, Nita 99995

July 18, YR-1

To whom it may concern:

Henry C. Fordyce was employed by this office on March 2, YR-1, when he was attending a conference on resource management at Nita City College. At the time, his job title was Senior Forest Ranger and his monthly gross salary was $7,000.

For the first month after his injury we were able to pay Mr. Fordyce because he had accumulated two weeks of sick leave and two weeks of vacation, both of which he used at that time. However, when those leaves were exhausted, we were obliged to grant Mr. Fordyce's request for personal leave without pay. For the months of April, May, and June, during which he would normally have been paid $21,000, he received no compensation.

Our hospitalization plan will take care of eighty percent of all of Mr. Fordyce's bills when they are submitted for payment. According to our records, those bills have not yet been submitted.

Please do not hesitate to contact me if you have any further questions.

Sincerely,

Richard C. Leeds

Richard C. Leeds

Personnel Manager

RCL/pam

Exhibit 3

Forest Service Internal Memo

United States Department of Agriculture
Forest Service

Nita Regional Office
Nita City, Nita 99995

MEMORANDUM

TO: Employee File of Henry Fordyce

FROM: T. Fleck, Supervisor *JF*

DATE: 10/10/YR-2

RE: Alleged Misconduct

Ranger Fordyce was accused this date of assault by Ranger Allen. Allen indicates Fordyce punched him several times after Allen said something to Fordyce about Leona Dagnit, a woman Fordyce sees socially. Allen denies provoking the fight. Fordyce says Allen implied Dagnit was immoral.

Controversy resolved internally with mutual apologies.

Exhibit 4

Police Report—Incident at Gus's Bar & Grill

Nita City Police Department			
Reporting Department			

1 AGENCY	2 IDENTIFIER – ORI	3 DATE	4 OCE FILE NO.
Nita City Police Dept.	NC 248/00/478	3/2/YR-1	0030607746-8NC

5 NARRATIVE

I was on foot patrol in the vicinity of 28th Street and Founders Boulevard. I was on special assignment in high crime area to show police visibility. At 11:00 p.m., I received a 911 report about a fight at Gus's Bar & Grill. I went to the premises and found four people involved—three men and one woman. I broke up the fight. No serious injuries; not clear who started fight. It appears that two men made loud remarks concerning the woman and a fight ensued. Insufficient information for arrest. Took names and addresses of participants and witnesses. At 11:10 p.m., I sent Felson and Harris out with a warning. Watched them leave in YR-3 red BMW sedan parked in the 2600 block of Founders Boulevard. Waited at Gus's until 11:20 p.m., then resumed foot patrol.

Participants:

      Edward Felson, DOB 2/8/YR-29, Eastern Motel, Nita City

      Gerald J. Harris, DOB 7/21/YR-28, 24 Wilson Street, Glendale, Nita

      Henry C. Fordyce, DOB 8/18/YR-25, 1421 Seminole Drive, Nita City

      Eva Marie Long, DOB 6/24/YR-26, 676 28th Street, Apt. 11B, Nita City

Witnesses:

      Melissa Angel, DOB 7/31/YR-27, 3056 Jackson Ave., Apt. 301, Nita City (bartender at Gus's Bar & Grill)

      James Nolan, DOB 1/6/YR-30, 14536 Davidson Pike, Nita City (cook at Gus's Bar & Grill)

6 OFFICER'S NAME	7 OFFICER'S SIGNATURE	8 DATE SUBMITTED	9 SUPERVISOR'S NAME	10
Peyton C. Logan	*Peyton C. Logan*	03/05/YR-1	Captain C. Davis	Page 1 of 1

Exhibit 5

Harris Arrest Report

Nita City Police Department
Reporting Department

1 AGENCY	2 AGENCY IDENTIFIER NO.		3 OCA FILE NO.	COURT STATUS		DISPOSITION	
Nita City PD	439/45/789		2126-03-06354-89	**4 PENDING**	**5 COMPLETE** XXX	**55 DATE** 3/19/YR-1	**56 COURT DOCKET** No. CR-3-586

5 NAME LAST	FIRST	MI	7 ALIAS/NICKNAME	57 COURT
Harris	Gerald	J	None	Nita City District Court Galloway, Judge

8 COMPLETE ADDRESS	9 PLACE OF BIRTH	
24 Wilson Street, Glendale, Nita 98265	Nita City, Nita	

10 RACE	11 SEX	12 AGE	13 DATE OF BIRTH	14 HEIGHT	15 WEIGHT	16 HAIR	17 EYES
Caucasian	M	27	7/21/YR-28	6'0"	175 lb	Brown	Hazel

18 COMPLEXION	19 MARRIED	20 OTHER DESCRIPTIVE INFORMATION	58 AS CHARGED	59 LESSER
Light	No			

21 PRINTS TAKEN	22 PHOTOGRAPH TAKEN	23 SOC. SEC. NO.	24 DRIVER LICENSE NO.	60 DISMISSED	61 ACQUITTED
Yes	Yes	XXX-XX-1184	Nita 38-36589	XXX	

25 EMPLOYER/SCHOOL	26 OCCUPATION	27 SCHOOL/WORK ADDRESS	62 SENTENCE
Sanders Cleaning	Owner	2608 Founders Blvd., Nita City, Nita 98266	

DETAILS OF ARREST

28 DATE ARRESTED	29 TIME OF ARREST	30 PLACE ARRESTED	
3/5/YR-1	2:00 p.m.	Place of business	

31 CHARGE(S)	32 UCR CODE
Assault with a deadly weapon	045

33 COMPLAINANT'S NAME AND ADDRESS
Henry Fordyce, 1421 Seminole Drive, Nita City,

34 WITH WARRANT	35 W/O WARRANT XXX	36 ON VIEW	37 SUMMONS	38 JUVENILE	39 DISP. OF JUVENILE

40 DATE OF FOFFENSE	41 TIME OF OFFENSE	42 LOCATION OF OFFENSE	63 OTHER – DESCRIBE
3/2/YR-1	11:30 p.m.	2700 block of Founders Blvd., Nita City, Nita 98267	

43 VEHICLE INFORMATION (YEAR, MAKE, MODEL, COLOR, LIC. NO., STATE)	44 PLACE VEHICLE STORED
N/A	N/A

BAIL INFORMATION

45 DATE	46 COURT	MAGISTRATE/JUDGE	47 TRIAL DATE
3/5/YR-1	District Court	Galloway	3/19/YR-1

48 BAIL AMOUNT	49 HELD ON BAIL	50 ROR	51 COMMITTED	52 COMMITTED W/O BAIL	53 PLACE COMMITTED
$5,000	XXX				

54 NARRATIVE	64 LEFT THUMB
At 11:35 p.m. heard screaming and returned to vicinity of Gus's Bar, 2847 Founder's Blvd., where previous incident occurred (see earlier report dated 3/2/YR-1). Saw subject, female, running toward me yelling, "He is killing my friend." Subject, Eva Marie Long, DOB 6/24/YR-26, had been involved in an earlier incident at the same location. I ran to location indicated by her—an alley between 27th and 28th streets on Founders Blvd. Found second subject involved in earlier fight in same location. Second subject appeared to have serious bodily injuries.	

66 OFFICER'S NAME	67 OFFICER'S SIGNATURE		68 DATE	65 RIGHT THUMB
Peyton C. Logan	*Peyton C. Logan*		3/5/YR-1	

69 SUPERVISOR'S SIGNATURE	70 RECORDED	71 ARRESTEE'S SIGNATURE	
Cap'n C. Davis	3/19/YR-1	*Gerald J. Harris*	

Case File

Exhibit 5(2)

Continuation Page

Nita City Police Department
Reporting Department

1 AGENCY	2 IDENTIFIER – ORI	3 CONFIGURATION TO	4 OCE FILE NO
Nita City Police Dept.	NC 439/45/789	☐ INVESTIGATION ☐ SUPPLEMENTARY INV.	2126-03-06354-89

5 NARRATIVE

3/2/YR-1: Henry C. Fordyce, DOB 8/18/YR-25, unconscious on sidewalk. Bleeding from head, nose, and ears. Called for ambulance and backup. Long and Fordyce went to hospital in ambulance. Photographed and collected stick/purse/wallet/phone in evidence bags. No surveillance cameras observed in alley. I followed ambulance to Memorial Hospital in watch commander's vehicle. At hospital, Long informed me that attackers in second fight were same as in earlier fight. Had notes from earlier investigation. Put out BOLO on Edward Felson, DOB 2/8/YR-29, and Gerald J. Harris, DOB 7/21/YR-28.

3/5/YR-1: Detectives brought in suspects Harris and Felson. Both arrested this date. Suspects given rights and placed in lineup. Seven men involved. Long originally identifies both Felson and Harris. Further questioning by detectives indicates Long not positive Felson was present at time of assault. Long now unsure two assailants were present in alley at time of assault. Will make weak witness. Victim still hospitalized, unable to participate in lineup. Bond set at $5,000 for both suspects. Suspect Harris released on bond. Suspect Felson detained.

3/6/YR-1: Investigation reveals no additional witnesses to alleged crime. Suspects make no statements on advice of counsel. At arraignment, this date, confirmed by Asst. DA that cases won't stick.

3/17/YR-1: Received report from Crime Lab. No usable prints on stick. Purse only had Long's prints. Blood on stick matches Fordyce.

3/19/YR-1: Case against both suspects dismissed. Suspect Felson released.

6 OFFICER'S NAME	7 OFFICER'S SIGNATURE	8 DATE SUBMITTED	9 SUPERVISOR'S NAME	10
Peyton C. Logan	*Peyton C. Logan*	03/19/YR-1	Captain C. Davis	Page 2 of 2

56   National Institute for Trial Advocacy

Exhibit 5(3)

Street Diagram

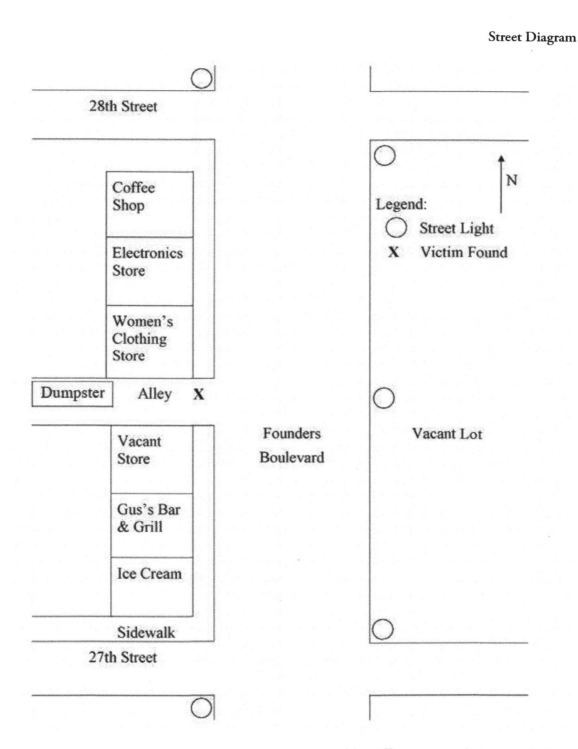

Prepared by Officer Peyton C. Logan, 3/5/YR-1

Exhibit 6

Felson Arrest Report

Nita City Police Department
Reporting Department

1 AGENCY Nita City PD	2 AGENCY IDENTIFIER NO. 439/45/789		3 OCA FILE NO. 2126-03-06354-89	COURT STATUS		DISPOSITION	
				4 PENDING	5 COMPLETE XXX	55 DATE 3/19/YR-1	56 COURT DOCKET No. CR-3-587

5 NAME	LAST Felson	FIRST Edward	MI W	7 ALIAS/NICKNAME None	57 COURT Nita City District Court Galloway, Judge

8 COMPLETE ADDRESS Eastern Motel, 2140 Hwy. 3, Nita City, Nita 98260	9 PLACE OF BIRTH Nita City, Nita	

10 RACE Caucasian	11 SEX M	12 AGE 29	13 DATE OF BIRTH 2/8/YR-29	14 HEIGHT 5'11"	15 WEIGHT 165 lb	16 HAIR Brown	17 EYES Brown	

18 COMPLEXION Dark	19 MARRIED No	20 OTHER DESCRIPTIVE INFORMATION	58 AS CHARGED	59 LESSER

21 PRINTS TAKEN Yes	22 PHOTOGRAPH TAKEN Yes	23 SOC. SEC. NO. XXX-XX-9183	24 DRIVER LICENSE NO. Nita 49-34143	60 DISMISSED XXX	61 ACQUITTED

25 EMPLOYER/SCHOOL Unemployed	26 OCCUPATION N/A	27 SCHOOL/WORK ADDRESS N/A	62 SENTENCE

DETAILS OF ARREST

28 DATE ARRESTED 3/5/YR-1	29 TIME OF ARREST 12:45 p.m.	30 PLACE ARRESTED Eastern Motel	

31 CHARGE(S) Assault with a deadly weapon	32 UCR CODE(S) 045

33 COMPLAINANT'S NAME AND ADDRESS Henry Fordyce, 1421 Seminole Drive, Nita City	

34 WITH WARRANT	35 W/O WARRANT XXX	36 ON VIEW	37 SUMMONS	38 JUVENILE	39 DISP. OF JUVENILE

40 DATE OF FOFFENSE 3/2/YR-1	41 TIME OF OFFENSE 11:30 p.m.	42 LOCATION OF OFFENSE 2700 block of Founders Blvd., Nita City, Nita 98267	63 OTHER – DESCRIBE

43 VEHICLE INFORMATION (YEAR, MAKE, MODEL, COLOR, LIC. NO., STATE) N/A	44 PLACE VEHICLE STORED N/A

BAIL INFORMATION

45 DATE 3/5/YR-1	46 COURT MAGISTRATE/JUDGE District Court Galloway	47 TRIAL DATE 3/19/YR-1

48 BAIL AMOUNT $5,000	49 HELD ON BAIL XXX	50 ROR	51 COMMITTED XXX	52 COMMITTED W/O BAIL	53 PLACE COMMITTED Nita City Jail

54 NARRATIVE See attached report for Gerald J. Harris, co-defendant.	64 LEFT THUMB

66 OFFICER'S NAME Peyton C. Logan	67 OFFICER'S SIGNATURE *Peyton C. Logan*	68 DATE 3/5/YR-1	65 RIGHT THUMB

69 SUPERVISOR'S SIGNATURE *Cap'n C. Davis*	70 RECORDED 3/19/YR-1	71 ARRESTEE'S SIGNATURE *Edward W. Felson*

Exhibit 7

Floor Layout of Gus's Bar & Grill

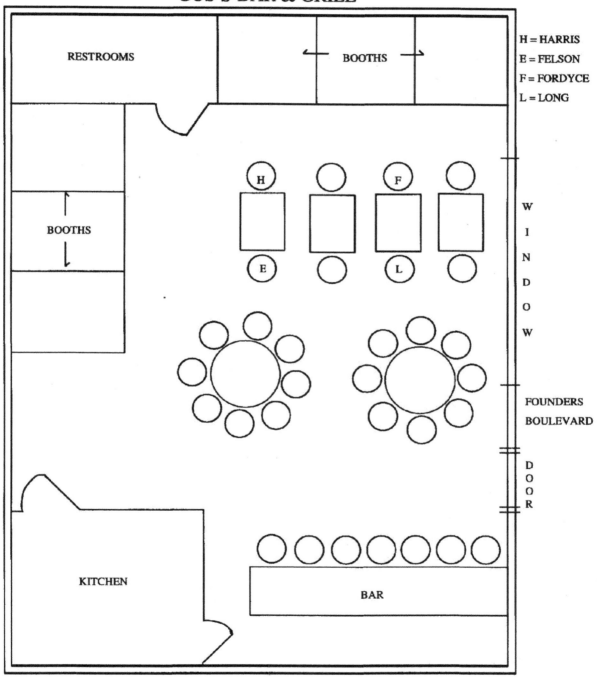

Exhibit 8

Nita City Streets

									N ↑
30th									
29th									
28th x	Arena		Long x						
27th			Gus's x						
26th				x Sander's Cleaning					→
25th									To
24th									Eastern
23rd									Motel
22nd									(.5 mile)
21st									
20th									
19th									
18th									
17th									
16th									
15th									
14th									
13th									
12th									
11th									
10th									
9th									
8th									
7th									
6th									
5th			x Barkan						
4th									
3rd									
2nd									
1st									

Jackson Avenue · Indiana Avenue · Holt Avenue · Grace Avenue · Founders Boulevard · Edison Concourse · Davidson Pike · Corona Avenue · Boulder Avenue

To Glendale ↓
(15 miles)

Exhibit 9

Henry Fordyce Arrest Record

UNIFORM ARREST AND DISPOSITION RECORD

NAME: S.S. NO:	Henry C. Fordyce XXX-XX-5756	DOB: POB:	8/18/YR-25 Nita City, Nita
DATE ARRESTED 3/8/YR-3 1/1/YR-3	ADDRESS RFD Rt 27 Wolf Creek, Nita RFD Rt 27 Wolf Creek, Nita	OFFENSE Drunk and disorderly Drunk and disorderly; Assault on a Police Officer	DISPOSITION Dismissed Dismissed

Alexander McConachie

Alexander McConachie
Superintendent of Documents

Certified as of this 1st day of October, YR-1.

Charlotte Noll

Charlotte Noll

Notary Public

Exhibit 10

Eva Marie Long Arrest Record

UNIFORM ARREST AND DISPOSITION RECORD

NAME:	Eva Marie Long	DOB:	6/24/YR-26
S.S. NO:	XXX-XX-4414	POB:	Racine, WI

DATE ARRESTED	ADDRESS	OFFENSE	DISPOSITION
1/17/YR-2	676 28th St. Nita City, Nita	Poss. w/int Cocaine (felony)	Dismissed
7/30/YR-2	676 28th St. Nita City, Nita	Poss. w/int Cocaine (felony)	Dismissed

Alexander McConachie

Alexander McConachie
Superintendent of Documents

Certified as of this 1st day of October, YR-1.

Charlotte Noll

Charlotte Noll

Notary Public

Exhibit 11

Gerald Harris Arrest Record

UNIFORM ARREST AND DISPOSITION RECORD

NAME:	Gerald J. Harris	DOB:	7/21/YR-28
S.S. NO:	XXX-XX-1184	POB:	Nita City, Nita

DATE ARRESTED	ADDRESS	OFFENSE	DISPOSITION
10/12/YR-14	4727 Holt Ave. Nita City, Nita	Purse Snatching	Released to custody of parents
12/3/YR-14	4727 Holt Ave. Nita City, Nita	Assault	Released to custody of parents
6/24/YR-13	4727 Holt Ave. Nita City, Nita	Assault	Adj. delinquent 1 yr. probation
8/12/YR-12	4727 Holt Ave. Nita City, Nita	Carrying Concealed Weapon	Adj. delinquent 2 yrs. probation
4/28/YR-11	4727 Holt Ave. Nita City, Nita	Assault w/Deadly Weapon	Probation violation 1 yr. Training School Released 12/20/YR-11
3/5/YR-1	4 Wilson St. Glendale, Nita	Assault w/Deadly Weapon	Dismissed

Alexander McConachie

Alexander McConachie
Superintendent of Documents

Certified as of this 1st day of October, YR-1.

Charlotte Noll

Charlotte Noll

Notary Public

Exhibit 12

Edward Felson Arrest Record

UNIFORM ARREST AND DISPOSITION RECORD

NAME:	Edward W. Felson	DOB:	2/8/YR-29
S.S. NO:	XXX-XX-9183	POB:	Hartford, Nita

DATE ARRESTED	ADDRESS	OFFENSE	DISPOSITION
1/12/YR-6	1020 N. Broad St. Philadelphia, PA	Disorderly Conduct (misdemeanor)	G/P $25.00 fine
8/14/YR-4	9529 Kenyon Ave. Nita City, Nita	Larceny/auto theft (felony)	Jury Trial Guilty/6 mos. State Prison
10/21/YR-3	9529 Kenyon Ave. Nita City, Nita	Assault (felony)	Dismissed
3/5/YR-1	Eastern Motel Nita City, Nita	Assault w/Deadly Weapon	Dismissed
7/10/YR-1	Eastern Motel Nita City, Nita	Armed Robbery (felony)	Pending

Alexander McConachie

Alexander McConachie
Superintendent of Documents

Certified as of this 1st day of October, YR-1.

Charlotte Noll

Charlotte Noll

Notary Public

Exhibit 13

Hospital Report of Eva Marie Long
MEMORIAL HOSPITAL

PATIENT: Eva Marie Long   DOB: June 24, YR-26
676 28th St.
Nita City, Nita

NOK: Mr. Joseph M. Long
2417 Pinecrest Drive
Montrose, Nita

EMPLOYER: Self-employed

INSURANCE: None   ADMITTED: 9/2/YR-1 1:05 a.m.

9/2/YR-1 1:05 a.m.	Patient brought to ER by friend who declined to give name. Friend reports victim had been using cocaine. Ordered blood and urine samples stat. Observation of depressed respiration, pulse, and B.P. Reports confirm initial diagnosis of cocaine overdose. Patient improved rapidly. Hospitalization not necessary. Released at 10:00 a.m. with instructions to return in the event of any future problems. B. Chakabarty, MD

Certified as a true and correct copy of permanent records of Memorial Hospital, Nita City, Nita.

Sherman Fox

Sherman Fox

Director, Medical Records

Photograph of Purse, Phone, and Wallet Near Dumpster

Photograph of Broomstick in Dumpster

Exhibit 16

Crime Lab Report

NITA DEPARTMENT OF PUBLIC SAFETY
Nita Police Department • Forensic Laboratory
999 Nita Boulevard
Nita City, Nita 99997
(555) 724-5775

Investigating Officer	Peyton C. Logan	pclogan@nitacitypd.gov
Supervisor	Captain C. Davis	cdavis@nitacitypd.gov
Evidence Technician	Courtney Nathan	cnathan@forensics.nitadps.gov

Laboratory Case Number:	6152901
Agency:	Nita City Police Department
Agency Case Number:	439/45/789
OCA File Number:	2126-03-06354-89

Suspects:	**Victims:**
Gerald J. Harris	Henry C. Fordyce
Edward W. Felson	Eva Marie Long

Offense:	**Date of Offense:**
Assault with Deadly Weapon	3/2/YR-1

Evidence Submitted

Item Number:	Description:	Examination Requested:
01	Purse	Fingerprints
02	Phone	Fingerprints
03	Wallet	Fingerprints
04	Stick	Fingerprints, blood

Chain of Custody

Item:	Received From:	Received By:	Date:	Disposition:	Date:
01–04	Evidence Room	C. Nathan	3/15/YR-1	Returned to Evidence Room	3/15/YR-1

Case Summary

Victims were attacked in an alley in the 2700 block of Founders Blvd., Nita City, at approximately 11:30 p.m. Victims identified suspects as attackers. Suspects used stick and feet to attack. Purse and contents were taken.

Analysis Results

Items 01–03:

NARRATIVE: Items 01, 02, and 03 were examined for the presence of fingerprints. Fingerprints were found on each item. Fingerprints were consistent with one person. No other usable prints were found, although smudges were present. Fingerprints were compared to database of Nita City Police Department.

RESULTS: Fingerprints identified as from Eva Marie Long, victim.

Item 04:

NARRATIVE: Item 04 was examined for the presence of blood and for fingerprints. No usable prints were found. Blood discovered on stick. Blood type AB+.

RESULTS: Blood type matches Henry Fordyce, victim. No DNA test necessary.

The undersigned does hereby certify under NITA STATUTES 546.701 that the above is a true and accurate copy of the results of the tests conducted.

Courtney Nathan
Forensic Scientist

3/17/YR-1
Date of Analysis

Exhibit 17

Text Messages from Eva Marie Long's Phone

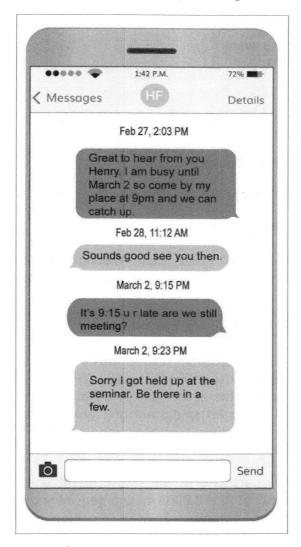

Nita Investigations, Inc.

495 Grace Blvd.
Nita City, Nita 99998
(555) 847-3851

CONFIDENTIAL REPORT

Prepared for: Plaintiff's Counsel

Prepared by: David Peterson, Nita Investigations, Inc.

Date: December 18, YR-1

Pursuant to your request, our office has investigated Gerald Harris's business, Sanders Cleaning Service, Inc., regarding possible overcharges on contracts with Nita City.

Our investigation reveals that Sanders had the contract for cleaning with the Nita City Department of Housing, which is located at 27 Smith Street. This contract commenced on July 1, YR-2, and was for a maximum term of three years. Each party had the option to renew for each year during the term. On June 1, YR-1, the Housing Authority wrote Mr. Harris, informing him that the contract would not be renewed and would instead terminate on June 30, YR-1. The letter did not give any reasons. Our informant in that office indicates that the Department of Housing believed they had been charged substantial sums for work that had not been performed.

On August 18, YR-1, the Department of Housing brought suit in Nita County Superior Court seeking repayment of $270,000 in alleged overcharges. The action was dismissed with prejudice on September 2, YR-1. Our informant further indicates that a settlement led to the dismissal and that, as a result of the settlement, Sanders Cleaning Services, Inc., paid the department $100,000.

Please do not hesitate to contact us if we can be of further assistance.

STATEMENT OF BEN SANDERS*
FEBRUARY 15, YR-0

My name is Ben Sanders, and I live at 1253 Melville Road, Glendale, Nita. I am sixty-eight years old and retired. I have been married to Alice Sanders for forty-seven years. We have three children and five grandchildren.

I have known Gerry Harris since he and my youngest son went to grade school together. My son Billy and Gerry were friends then, although they later went to different junior high schools. Gerry began to hang out with the wrong crowd and got into trouble. I coached my son's baseball team and needed a catcher, and I knew Gerry could play, so I asked him to play on my son's team. Maybe I could help turn him around. I think it helped.

After high school, Gerry came to work for me. He quickly learned the business and became very knowledgeable about the whole operation—hiring, finances, customer relations, contracts. My own sons never wanted to learn the business, so Gerry became my "business" son. After a few years, Gerry approached me to buy the business. At first I was concerned, because this business is based on personal contacts, reputation, and goodwill, but Gerry had proven himself. Since I was looking to retire, I agreed to sell it to him in YR-3. He pays me yearly out of net earnings. He currently owes $225,000 on the note.

In my contacts with Gerry, I have known him to be a fine man not easily angered or inclined to use profanity. He has been in situations where another man might have lost his temper, but he didn't. He also does not drink to excess. I have never seen him drunk in any business or personal situation. He has a steady girlfriend, Glenda Barkan, and they come to our house for dinner often. I think they will marry soon.

I know he was arrested for a fight a Gus's Bar, but I know he didn't start it. Gus's is a little rough-and-tumble place near the office. Eddie Felson was there, and it is more likely that Felson was involved. He was a violent kid in high school.

Gerry would never have ambushed the guy outside the bar. He is not that kind of person. In my community, he has the reputation of being honest, law-abiding, and even-tempered. I know because I asked around.

Ben Sanders
Ben Sanders

---

* This statement was given to the defense attorney and provided to the plaintiff's counsel by defense counsel.

JURY INSTRUCTIONS

PART I

PRELIMINARY INSTRUCTIONS
GIVEN PRIOR TO THE EVIDENCE

1. Nita Preliminary Instruction 01:01 Introduction

You have been selected as jurors and have taken an oath to well and truly try this cause. This trial will last one day.

During the progress of the trial, there will be periods of time when the court recesses. During those periods of time, you must not talk about this case among yourselves or with anyone else.

During the trial, do not talk to any of the parties, their lawyers, or any of the witnesses.

If anyone attempts to talk to you concerning the matters here under consideration, you should immediately report that fact to the court.

You should keep an open mind. You should not form or express an opinion during the trial and should reach no conclusion in this case until you have heard all of the evidence, the arguments of counsel, and the final instructions as to the law that will be given to you by the court.

2. Nita Preliminary Instruction 01:02 Conduct of the Trial

First, the attorneys will have an opportunity to make opening statements. These statements are not evidence and should be considered only as a preview of what the attorneys expect the evidence will be.

Following the opening statements, witnesses will be called to testify. They will be placed under oath and questioned by the attorneys. Documents and other tangible exhibits may also be received as evidence. If an exhibit is given to you to examine, you should examine it carefully, individually, and without any comment.

It is counsel's right and duty to object when testimony or other evidence is being offered that he or she believes is not admissible.

When the court sustains an objection to a question, the jurors must disregard the question and the answer, if one has been given, and draw no inference from the question or answer or speculate as to what the witness would have said if permitted to answer. Jurors must also disregard evidence stricken from the record.

When the court sustains an objection to any evidence the jurors must disregard that evidence.

When the court overrules an objection to any evidence, the jurors must not give that evidence any more weight than if the objection had not been made.

When the evidence is completed, the attorneys will make closing arguments. These final statements are not evidence, but are given to assist you in evaluating the evidence. The attorneys are also permitted to argue in an attempt to persuade you to a particular verdict. You may accept or reject those arguments as you see fit.

Finally, just before you retire to consider your verdict, the court will give you further instructions on the law that applies to this case.

PART II

FINAL INSTRUCTIONS

3. Nita Instruction 1:01 Introduction

Members of the jury, the evidence and arguments in this case have been completed, and I will now instruct you as to the law.

The law applicable to this case is stated in these instructions, and it is your duty to follow all of them. You must not single out certain instructions and disregard others.

It is your duty to determine the facts and to determine them only from the evidence in this case. You are to apply the law to the facts and in this way decide the case. You must not be governed or influenced by sympathy or prejudice for or against any party in this case. Your verdict must be based on evidence and not on speculation, guess, or conjecture.

From time to time the court has ruled on the admissibility of evidence. You must not concern yourselves with the reasons for these rulings. You should disregard questions and exhibits that were withdrawn or to which objections were sustained.

You should also disregard testimony and exhibits that the court has refused or stricken.

The evidence that you should consider consists only of the witnesses' testimonies and the exhibits the court has received.

Any evidence that was received for a limited purpose should not be considered by you for any other purpose.

You should consider all the evidence in the light of your own observations and experiences in life.

Neither by these instructions nor by any ruling or remark that I have made do I mean to indicate any opinion as to the facts or as to what your verdict should be.

4. Nita Instruction 1:02 Opening Statements and Closing Arguments

Opening statements are made by the attorneys to acquaint you with the facts they expect to prove. Closing arguments are made by the attorneys to discuss the facts and circumstances in the case, and should be confined to the evidence and to reasonable inferences to be drawn from it. Neither opening statements nor closing arguments are evidence, and any statement or argument made by the attorneys that is not based on the evidence should be disregarded.

5. Nita Instruction 1:03 Credibility of Witnesses

You are the sole judges of the credibility of the witnesses and of the weight to be given to the testimony of each witness. In determining what credit is to be given any witness, you may take into account their ability and opportunity to observe; their manner and appearance while testifying; any interest, bias, or prejudice they may have; the reasonableness of their testimony considered in the light of all the evidence; and any other factors that bear on the believability and weight of the witness's testimony.

6. Nita Instruction 1:05 Direct and Circumstantial Evidence

The law recognizes two kinds of evidence: direct and circumstantial. Direct evidence proves a fact directly; that is, the evidence by itself, if true, establishes the fact. Circumstantial evidence is the proof of facts or circumstances that give rise to a reasonable inference of other facts; that is, circumstantial evidence proves a fact indirectly in that it follows from other facts or circumstances according to common experience and observations in life. An eyewitness is a common example of direct evidence, while human footprints are circumstantial evidence that a person was present.

The law makes no distinction between direct and circumstantial evidence as to the degree or amount of proof required, and each should be considered according to whatever weight or value it may have. All of the evidence should be considered and evaluated by you in arriving at your verdict.

7. Nita Instruction 2:01 Burden of Proof

When I say that a party has the burden of proof on any issue, or use the expression "if you find," "if you decide," or "by a preponderance of the evidence," I mean that you must be persuaded from a consideration of all the evidence in the case that the issue in question is more probably true than not true.

Any findings of fact you make must be based on probabilities, not possibilities. It may not be based on surmise, speculation, or conjecture.

8. In order for the plaintiff, Mr. Fordyce, to recover from the defendants, Mr. Felson and Mr. Harris, on his claim of assault and battery, you must find that the following propositions have been established:

(a) One or both of the defendants acted with the intent of making a harmful or offensive contact with the plaintiff's person.

(b) One or both of the defendants' conduct resulted in a harmful or offensive contact with the person of the plaintiff.

(c) The harmful or offensive contact proximately caused the plaintiff's injuries.

If you find that any of these propositions has not been established by a preponderance of the evidence, then your verdict must be for the defendants.

If, on the other hand, you find that all of these propositions have been established by a preponderance of the evidence, then your verdict must be for the plaintiff.

There are two defendants in this case, Mr. Felson and Mr. Harris, and the evidence should be considered with respect to each of them. You must reach a verdict as to each defendant.

9. Assault and battery is defined as harmful or offensive contact with another person. A contact is the intentional touching of another. A harmful contact is one that causes physical pain, injury, or illness. An offensive contact is one that would offend another's reasonable sense of personal dignity.

10. A person intends to commit an assault and battery if he acts for the purpose of making a harmful or offensive contact with another person.

11. Proximate cause means a cause that, in a natural and probable sequence, produced the alleged injury. It is a cause without which the claimed injury would not have been sustained.

12. Words alone do not justify an assault and battery and neither of the defendants, Mr. Felson or Mr. Harris, would be justified in committing an assault and battery on Mr. Fordyce solely because of any words that were used by any of the parties.

13. Do not infer from an instruction by the court on measure of damages that the court is instructing you to assess or not to assess damages. The question of whether or not to assess damages is a question for the jury's consideration.

14. Difficulty or uncertainty in ascertaining or measuring the precise amount of any damages does not preclude recovery; use your best judgment in determining the amount of such damages, if any, based on the evidence.

15. If you find in favor of the plaintiff, Mr. Fordyce, on his claim of assault and battery, then you must assess his damages, which may be actual or nominal.

To assess any actual damages, you must find from a preponderance of the evidence that the plaintiff sustained actual damages as a proximate result of the claimed battery.

To the extent that any actual damages have been so established by the evidence, you shall assess, as the plaintiff's actual damages, an amount that will fairly and justly compensate him for:

(a) Any reasonable expenses he may have incurred for medical expenses;

(b) Any loss of earnings he may have sustained;

(c) Any pain and suffering, physical discomfort, or inconveniences he may have sustained;

(d) Any physical illness or injury he may have sustained; and

(e) Any emotional distress, fear, anxiety, embarrassment, humiliation, or loss of reputation he may have sustained.

If you find in favor of the plaintiff, but do not find any actual damages, you shall nonetheless award him nominal damages in the sum of one dollar.

16. If you find in favor of the plaintiff, Mr. Fordyce, on the issue of actual or nominal damages, you may also consider whether the actions of the defendant or defendants were malicious. Malicious means that the defendant or defendants acted without regard to the life, liberty, or safety of the plaintiff and with the specific intent to cause serious life-threatening injury. If you determine that the defendant or defendants acted maliciously, you may award additional damages designed to punish the defendant or defendants for their actions and deter him/them from acting in a similar way in the future.

17. Nita Instruction 1:06 Concluding Instruction

The court did not in any way and does not by these instructions give or intimate any opinions as to what has or has not been proven in the case, or as to what are or are not the facts of the case.

No one of these instructions states all of the law applicable, but all of them must be taken, read, and considered together as they are connected with and related to each other as a whole.

You must not be concerned with the wisdom of any rule of law. Regardless of any opinions you may have as to what the law ought to be, it would be a violation of your sworn duty to base a verdict on any other view of the law than that given in the instructions of the court.

IN THE SUPERIOR COURT OF
DARROW COUNTY, NITA
CIVIL DIVISION

HENRY C. FORDYCE,   )

Plaintiff,   )

v.   )   FORM OF VERDICT

GERALD J. HARRIS and   )   487-CV-1253
EDWARD FELSON,   )

Defendants.   )

WE, THE JURY, AND EACH OF US FIND:

COMPENSATORY DAMAGES

(Circle one and fill in appropriate amount)

I.   For the plaintiff in the amount of $ _____ against both defendants.

II.   For the plaintiff in the amount of $ _____ and against only defendant Felson.

III.   For the plaintiff in the amount of $ _____ and against only defendant Harris.

IV.   For the defendants.

PUNITIVE DAMAGES

(Only if you have circled I, II, or III above, choose either V/VI below OR VII.)

V.   For the plaintiff and against defendant Felson in the amount of $ _____.

VI.   For the plaintiff and against defendant Harris in the amount of $ _____.

VII.   No punitive damages.

IN THIS VERDICT EACH OF US CONCURS.

_____   _____
Foreperson   Date